i

c

o

p

e

YOUNG AMERI CANS

JORDA N CAS TRO

CONTENTS

i want to do something   (11)
i want to lecture your mom   (15)
bdsm   (19)
professional actor   (23)
things i've never done   (27)
post mom suicide tweet poem   (31)
on feeling better after feeling badly   (35)
unchill   (39)
young americans   (43)
extremely high in a dark ass room   (47)
something weird just happened and i felt really sad   (53)
it is my fault that i feel alone   (57)
help me   (61)
i live at my parents' house   (65)
comments, likes, and reblogs   (69)
selections from jordan castro's twitter account 4.19.09 - 8.23.10, edited by mallory whitten   (73)
i'm sorry i get mad and talk in an irritated tone of voice to you   (77)
haiku for growing apart   (81)
salad   (85)
incredibly uncomfortable   (89)
saturday morning, what should i do   (93)
poem i wrote while pooping after eating an entire box of vegan chicken nuggets at your house then edited a little later while listening to your guitar solo (97)
ewyfs   (101)

willing (105)
insomnia (109)
melatonin (113)
(bi)polar bear! (117)
haiku for drugs (121)
adhd (125)
haiku for taking one's time and trying to be chill (129)
selections from jordan castro's twitter account 5.29.6
- 9.2.11, edited by megan boyle (133)
intro to human communication (139)
dorm room terror (143)
'photo booth' video emotional poem (147)
10.10.11. 5:30AM (151)
raymond carver's *what we talk about when we talk about love* (the story) or dennis cooper's *ugly man* (the book) (155)
granola bar sorrow (159)
the social network (163)
11.13.92 (167)
11.15.10 (171)
11.22.10 (175)
hamlet ass pancakes (179)
'paper planes' by m.i.a. (183)
eating disorder (187)
you guys know shrimp, right? well shrimp, you know, they keep everything to themselves. like, they don't give to charity or anything. well the other day, my friend, he told me, he said 'you know why shrimp are like that, don'tcha?' i told him, i said, 'no clue, why are they like that?' he told me, he said 'because they're *shellfish*' (191)
'american psycho' (195)
'second marriage' (199)

can't stop thinking that people are probably inherently
fucked and other things about the bleakness of the
universe   (203)
pooping in public restrooms   (207)
haiku for pooping during class   (211)
sad americans   (215)
apple cider   (219)
haiku for monday morning   (223)
i don't feel comfortable around you anymore   (227)
unbearable   (231)
allergic to peanuts   (235)
old man back   (239)

I WANT
TO DO
SOMETHING

i don't think i want to be writing a poem right now

i think i want to feel the illusion of productivity

without having to think about what i'm actually doing

or something

i want to forget everything i've ever learned about poetry

then write a poem

or translate street rap lyrics into 'perfect english'

then sell it

but either way

i want to do something that isn't a lot of specific things

or something

like be a cop

or kill myself

or go to sleep

or something

I WANT TO LECTURE YOUR MOM

in a well-organized, meticulous e-mail

i want to tell your mom that she is bad

utilizing a tone of voice that (while still seeming, to some degree, like
my natural tone of voice) adequately expresses a degree of
empathy toward her while simultaneously stating objective facts
re 'what she does on an average day,' 'the effects of a mother
and a family on a child,' 'what she needs to do to ensure a
healthy childhood and adolescence for her children and how
she's not currently doing that,' and that your mom is a retarded
asshole

i want to conclude the email by telling your mom that she has two
options

she can either

a.) feel upset or angry or something, sulk, bitch, smoke cigarettes,
look at facebook, etc
or
b.) change in a manner that will increase the quality of her and her
children's lives

and i want her to choose option b

and i want you to feel happy and comfortable at home

and grow healthily

into something that isn't something else

that's worse than what you could have been

or something

BDSM

i want to punch people who unsarcastically believe in 'right' and
   'wrong' in the face

with my fist

the fist of indifference

i want to destroy everyone

and watch as they cower in fear

fear of the horrible things i am capable of

because morals mean nothing when there's a knife to your throat

and you can't talk shit with a gun in your mouth

i want to detach every single limb that is currently attached to every
   single human on earth

except for their heads and their hands

so they can visit my blog

and compliment me via comment

and tell me how good i am for being so young

and smile

and give me 'mad hits'

and unsolicited blowjobs when i meet them in real life

i want to say sentences like

'anything can be made to have meaning

depending on one's context and goal'

and 'anything can cause any kind of response

because the response is not caused by the thing but by the person
perceiving the thing'

i want something to happen but i don't know what that something is

so i sit here and complain and i don't stop until the drugs kick in

PROFES-
SIONAL
ACTOR

i don't understand what the days have to do with me

i spend the time i enjoy writing, on drugs, or writing while on drugs

in an attempt to rid myself of the day

and the day of myself

i don't understand what people want from me

i honestly feel like i have nothing to give to them

people want illusions – facial expressions, camera angles, lighting
— when the truth is an unlit monotony, seen from one angle, and
the angle is not of your choosing

or something

i don't know...

things happen

and other things happen

you are there and i am here

refreshing twitter at an alarmingly high frequency

alone

in bed

at 5AM

for a moment i consider tweeting something

then don't tweet anything

there is nothing i can tweet right now to alleviate my acute feelings of
   alienation, depression, confusion and despair

if for no other reason than the line before this one

all lines before that one

etc

THINGS I'VE NEVER DONE

i've never lived in an impoverished neighborhood

i've never lived anywhere outside of northeast ohio

the united states of america

i've never not been allergic to peanuts, shellfish, and other things

i've never not loved my enemies

i've never been diagnosed with cancer

i've never not had cancer

i've never killed a human being

on purpose or immediately

POST MOM SUICIDE TWEET POEM

after imagining [person]'s mom killing herself, i thought about
     whether [person] sh/would tweet 'my mom just killed herself' or
     'my mom just killed herself...'

ON FEELING BETTER AFTER FEELING BADLY

sometimes

there is nothing

a person can say

or do

to help

UNCHILL

i've never really considered myself 'unchill' as like, a personality
thing, but it seems to me, now more than ever, that in a lot of
situations i do, in fact, say and do some pretty 'unchill' things

YOUNG
AMERICANS

i feel incredibly high

after ingesting adderall, marijuana, vicoprofen, and alcohol

and linking a recent publication on my twitter feed

while sam, sitting near me, draws something that i only feel able to
describe as 'fucking bad ass'

or 'fucking sweet'

or something

*

yesterday i felt incredibly high

after ingesting adderall, mdma, marijuana, and alcohol

at the alamo

with writers and gay people

and three cats

and dubstep music

i hallucinated cartoon-like images after closing my eyes before sleep

my vision and body felt like they were continually 'moving forward' in
a castle

laser beams repeatedly 'shot out' of my peripherals into the distance
in front of my face

i saw a well overflow with water in a wave-like manner then fire
'shoot out' of it then lava flow toward my face

at some point, an overweight, drunk man with a southern accent
    walked into the room, pointed at everyone individually then said,
    'okay this is a test you guys. who's this song by?'

someone said 'phish'

someone said something else

i repeatedly thought 'travis pastrana'

someone said a name i'd never heard before

the drunk man said 'joe walsh' while laughing very loudly

EXTREMELY HIGH IN A DARK ASS ROOM

felt a desire to 'create something,' i think, or 'write down' 'this
    moment' so i can remember it or 'use it' for art

didn't want to anything, i don't know

decided to 'resign' to emailing you after vision began blurring

vision is almost entirely blurred

it feels like i'm staring blankly through the eyes of a smaller head
    within my head, through 'the screen' of my 'outer face'

like my hands and the laptop feel very far away

it feels like i'm wearing a headband but i'm not

ziggy and evan are sleeping

ate 3x packet 'gusher's' & 2x packet 'scooby doo' gummies

still seem to feel the sugar on my teeth...

i am squinting

my legs feel like...enormous and warm and tingly

a blowjob would be good right now

'this is the time for a blowjob,' i think as i squint my eyes at the
    screen and feel nauseous

i just closed my eyes and allowed my head to 'roll back,' hitting the
    wall

just...did it again on accident

just saw the word 'YES' flash in front of my eyes in pink neon
    lettering my blinking feels slow and 'fuzzy'

feel paralyzed and retarded a little

just thought 'analyze me past now bitch!' in an irish accent, i think

my body feels slow...everything is moving slowly

just thought 'i don't know what is going on at any given moment,
    none of us do' in a manner like i was thinking of myself saying it,
    i think

kekekkalooooooooo nigga!!!

nigga nigga fuh cakaka cooky lala boondychacha

things don't feel easier or better, in slow motion, they just feel
    different

i feel like i'm breathing underwater, or being born, maybe

i feel like i can go many hours without thinking about anybody but
    myself and maybe mallory

or like days or maybe weeks

i don't know

bricksquad, bricksquad – everything is bricksquad

i feel like a rap star

my life this past week has felt like a rap star's life, a little, i think

stared blankly for ~1 min then 'realized' i was thinking [something i
    just forgot....tried to remember for ~2 min]

mass confusion

forgot a lot of things about my life, like, it feels like only a really small
    portion of things gets remembered, like... i don't know, nothing
    like, makes me sad anymore, like, that used to make me sad
    ('mad me' sad./..)

i feel like a struggling like, fish or something

sorry i typed so much

keep thinking something like 'i'm so high' then 'what the fuck' or
    'where the fuck' or [something else]

SOMETHING WEIRD JUST HAPPENED AND I FELT REALLY SAD

i experienced a strange despair

after imagining my dad

alone

in bed

crying and touching his face

pulling at his nonexistent hair

repeatedly saying 'i just want to be a fun, creative uncle'

and 'why doesn't my family appreciate me'

i stood

staring blankly

for around 3 minutes

feeling this feeling take hold

sink into me like some

thing sinking in to me

IT IS MY FAULT THAT I FEEL SAD

just thought 'i wish everyone was a porn star' while looking at a
female i've seen at school infrequently since fifth grade

i haven't masturbated in days

the chances of me ever actually pursuing an attractive female that
doesn't express interest in me first seem slim to none

'at this point'

the chances of me ever actually pursuing an attractive female in
general seem slim to none

the illusions that used to excite me no longer excite me

because they no longer exist

i can't talk to people

boring, inconsiderate

i don't know

people are fine

if i can't interact with them it's because i don't know how to

it is my fault that i feel alone

and if everyone were a porn star

i'm sure i'd wish the opposite

HELP ME

i want you to be green on gmail chat
when i want you to be green on gmail chat
and i want to convey certain thoughts/emotions
with an endearing lack of precision

and i want you to want to help me
because, you know, i'm oh so sad and lonely

by petting my head, giving me drugs
letting our legs touch while smoking cigarettes

i will feel less empty
but never more full
like the first few minutes after eating a bagel

the thought of another
like being 'bro-iced'

full of shit but full of something at least

i want you to want to help me but
i want to remain, for the most part, without help

the only thing i remember from last night
reaching desperately for my phone
to text you

to tell you i was throwing up
because of pills

when what i wanted to say -
what i've always wanted to say -
was

'i like you a lot and i miss you,
goodnight'

I LIVE AT MY PARENTS' HOUSE

i just woke up

i am going to eat oatmeal now

drink coffee

i had a dream about waking up and checking my blog

seeing nine comments

there hasn't been a new comment on my blog for the past seven
    hours

COMMENTS, LIKES, AND REBLOGS

just uploaded music to bandcamp.com

then linked it on twitter, tumblr, blogger, and facebook

while listening to a song by defiance, ohio on repeat

in bed

alone

waiting for the comments, likes, and reblogs

to start rollin' in

to slowly alleviate my steadily declining self-esteem

self-confidence

self

a friend who moved to south korea messages me on gmail chat

i list the drugs i'm on
she tells me that she's worried
she tells me that i need to slow down sometimes
i thank her and apologize

i am plagued by the problems i've created for myself

worse every second i'm alive

always trying, rarely doing

waiting for the comments, likes, and reblogs

for anything, really

still waiting

SELECTIONS FROM JORDAN CASTRO'S TWITTER ACCOUNT 4.19.09 – 8.23.10, EDITED BY MALLORY WHITTEN

10:54PM Sep 19
internet just closed 'out of nowhere,' felt my face go from neutral to
'intense agony/disbelief' to neutral in ~3 seconds

8:41PM Feb 10
my parents found my twitter account...dad threatened to 'turn off the
internet' if i didn't [something]...

4:35PM Feb 12
dreamt i 'scurried' through a shantytown in india, frantically asking the
vendors for '45 weapons'

10:01PM Feb 25
thought 'who should i kill next,' while shirtless/looking at myself in the
mirror/brushing my teeth

10:26PM Mar 10
'whipped my dick out' while brushing my teeth, looked at it in the mirror
a little, maintained a neutral facial expression

12:02PM May 2
repeatedly/calmly thought, 'damn re lower class,' while referring to lower
case letters, i think, while standing in the shower

11:26AM Jun 19
repeatedly thought, 'really disappointed via lack of stimulants,' while 'un
numbing' my ass/legs via 'shaking motions' after >25 min. poop

1:03PM Jun 19
repeatedly/in a tone and rhythm maybe 'akin' to 'run d.m.c.' or 'the beas-
tie boys' thought, 'little italy brand pizza sauce'

12:24PM Jul 1
looked at 'ghetto black girls' myspace pictures ~10 min experiencing
high interest levels & (what i hoped to be) ~70% 'unrelated boner'...

3:27PM Jul 9
unsarcastically felt myself thinking, 'life is so hard,' while taking a break
from editing my poetry book to put away/count my money

12:11AM Aug 10
absentmindedly 'jacked off my limp penis' while scrolling through gmail,
'completely unaware that i was "jacking off"' ~15 sec...

12:13PM Aug 20
got out of shower & honestly couldn't remember whether or not i 'condi-
tioned' my hair, got back in shower after ~3 min & 'conditioned'...

11:45AM Aug 23
feels like i am floating in an 'orb made of jelly...'a jelly orb...' i feel...'i feel
like i am slowly descending in a jelly orb...'

I'M SORRY
I GET MAD
AND TALK IN
AN
IRRITATED
TONE OF
VOICE TO
YOU

'you seem happier around other people,' you say

'you never have emotional conflicts with other people like you do
     with me'

'obviously i don't have emotional conflicts with other people like i do
     with you,' i say

'because i don't care about them as much as i care about you'

i think about my tone of voice, how i shouldn't be talking to you the
     way i'm talking to you now

i think about how i shouldn't feel frustrated about you feeling worried
     that i don't like you as much as you like me, how just because i
     feel like that's not true doesn't mean i do an adequate job of
     expressing my feelings to you, and how it's partially my fault that
     you feel the way you feel

i think about how i should understand that power exists in relation
     ships and that in this case - in this specific, isolated incident - i
     have more power than you and i'm abusing that power by talking
     in an irritated tone of voice, which is unproductive and a dick-
     move on my part

i think vaguely about your father

then sigh

like a dumb ass

after taking pills

drinking beer

and smoking weed

at 12:41PM

communicating nothing

except my faults and my inability to treat you how you deserve to be
   treated

i'm sorry

HAIKU FOR GROWING APART

the distance between
us like continental drift
gradual and vast

SALAD

walking down stairs

putting spinach, black olives, carrots, cucumbers, celery, sunflower seeds, and dried cranberries into a bowl

squeezing a lemon over the bowl

moving pieces of the bowl's contents toward my face with a fork

remembering that time i put my ear against your head while you were eating chips and i could hear the crunching and the crunching was amplified

INCREDIBLY UNCOMFORT-ABLE

you know you're fucked when the number of times you've
   masturbated in the past 48 hours is greater than the number of
   hours you've slept

true worthlessness is calling everyone you know and the only one
   who answers if your drug dealer

i feel incredibly uncomfortable

i somehow manage to always feel incredibly uncomfortable

no matter what

if i had a superpower, that would be my superpower

feeling incredibly uncomfortable all the time no matter what

they'd call me 'incredibly uncomfortable man'

god damn it...

'i will never sleep for longer than five hours without the help of drugs
   for the rest of my life' is causing high-level anxiety at 5:30AM,
   making it harder to sleep, causing high-level anxiety about my
   high-level anxiety about not being able to sleep, etc

i have spent too many nights lying in bed feeling crushed

crippled by the demands of the universe, my body, my brain

i don't know what to do

except keep working

until i have enough money to consistently have the drugs i need to
   sleep

until i have a girlfriend and no longer need to masturbate

until i die and my anxiety evaporates

not into the water cycle or anything

just gone or whatever

SATURDAY MORNING, WHAT SHOULD I DO

there is something about fat people falling that causes me to type 'fat people falling' into the search bar on youtube.com

anticipating good feelings

in eighth grade i typed 'gag' into the search bar on xvideos.com

my favorite songs include 'the moon will rise' by ghost mice and

'aside' by the weakerthans

i listen to rap music loudly

while delivering pizzas

in the car that my parents lent me

POEM I WROTE WHILE POOPING AFTER EATING AN ENTIRE BOX OF VEGAN CHICKEN NUGGETS AT YOUR HOUSE THEN EDITED A LITTLE LATER WHILE LISTENING TO YOUR GUITAR SOLO

i feel like the back of my head is being stabbed repeatedly by little
    knives that were already inside of my head before the stabbing

i feel like it'll last forever

i feel physical and mental weakness like i'd imagine a lizard would
    feel in the middle of january or july

i feel like a lizard...

i feel warmth in my face and it feels like a fever or something else
    shitty
a perverted uncle
an unwelcome acquaintance in a group of close friends
a close friend

i feel like my throat is a hamster cage at 'pet smart'
all hamster cages
all hamsters
all cages

and there exists only throat lozenges and drugs

to temporarily divert attention

i feel like adderall is the version of me that should be talking to other
    people and alcohol is the version of me that should be killing
    other people or myself

i feel like that sentence doesn't mean anything but neither do i

and i feel like that's okay

in an effort to temporarily divert attention

i will write this poem and read it

with a neutral facial expression

touch my moustache

move words around

edit it

i don't know

i feel like shit

i feel like my skull is a zoo and the animals are running rampant
  because the zookeeper of my brain thought it would be a good
  idea to release them and i feel like it will realize too late that a
  free animal is a dangerous animal

i feel like a more belligerent version of myself, typing similes to
  convey sentiments and starting every sentence with 'i feel like'

i just thought of a novel called 'the hangover' in a manner like i could
  write a novel called 'the hangover' then remembered the movie
  'the hangover' and felt something like a puddle, i think

EWYFS

the only honest response i can think of to the question 'how are you feeling?' is

'ready to punch the next person who asks me how i'm feeling in the face'

unfortunately

i can't stop thinking, saying, doing

certain things

'uh...' for example

'finna' for example

'drugs' for example

and i know there is a large portion of my being that you hate

and that this is the only reason i can think of for acting the way that i act when i'm around you

there is no amount of information that can make a person smarter, only an amount of information that can cause a person to think that s/he knows a certain amount of information

it's time that we start acting like ourselves again

crying when we're hungry and eating when we're sad

WILLING

i feel like a b grade actor trying to 'salvage my career' by taking any opportunity i get to pretend i'm someone else

i don't do enough nice things for the people i care about but from now on i'm going to do more – hopefully enough - nice things for them

it will never be possible to do enough nice things for a person

after ingesting 3mg xanax, 5 beers, 2 shots of whiskey, and smoking weed for the first time in what feels like forever -

i think about a broken down greyhound and the person i was

rest stop, legs, hands, shaking with the knowledge that my brain, heart exist unhappily inside of my skin

friends
family
future
me

'i miss you' means we're not together

'i'm sorry' means you were right and it matters

'i promise' means i can't right now

and the future is a lie

and i can't predict the future

and when you encouraged me to get help from a doctor or a therapist, i immediately said no

not because it wouldn't help (i can't say, i never tried) - and not because i believe that my friends and i can do it - but because, in all honesty, i'm not sure how willing i am to get better

to change

INSOMNIA

i can't sleep

it seems insane to be expected to lie in a dark room alone and not
    feel completely crazy and bipolar and confused and more awake

nighttime is my mirror

and i don't know how to face it

MELATONIN

while falling asleep

i feel a certain sense of 'giving up'

a certain sense of loss

something like investing money

(BI)POLAR BEAR!

i lie down with myself(s) after another day –
the result of days, all days
before it –
and close my eyes

try to sleep

after a period of time

i notice myself thinking in what seem to be two entirely different
    thought processes

my brain illustrating again what seems to be an uncanny ability to
    create multiple layers of consciousness

recently i've been doing this thing where i think something then think
    'just thought [thought]' then 'just thought "just thought [thought]"'
    for a period of time until something else happens

i don't know

most days i earnestly believe that there is nothing to believe in

while trying to sleep

a sweaty, obese anxiety crawls into bed with me

cuddles with me
tickles me
punches me
kicks me
then smiles

'you will never have enough money to legitimately support yourself'

'even the people who think they like you only like a part of you, or their
    perception of a part of you rather, and they don't know how much of
    a piece of shit you are beneath your stupid clothes and your retarded
    facial hair. you're the worst and you know it. deserving of nothing
    less than torture. a counterfeit dollar or a flat tire. a piece of horrible
    shit in the toilet of the world that needs to be flushed immediately but

won't be flushed immediately because suffering and lying and being a bitch is its sole reason for existing and it needs to remain afloat in order to do those things'

'no one loves you'

while rap music plays loudly from somewhere inside of me

and i listen to that too

HAIKU FOR DRUGS

if only i could
have constant access to all
my favorite drugs

ADHD

online, i read a review of focalin xr that said it 'stimulates [one's] peripherals' more than adderall does

seemed really strange, to me, to think about the stimulation of one's peripheral vision

HAIKU FOR TAKING ONE'S TIME AND TRYING TO BE CHILL

everything seems rushed
i mean, like, yeah, i don't know
down for whatever

SELECTIONS FROM JORDAN CASTRO'S TWITTER ACCOUNT 5.29.6 – 9.2.11, EDITED BY MEGAN BOYLE

1:39PM May 6
just finished my last day of high school

10:43PM May 11
perceived @mallory_whitten from a distance larger than the actual distance between us and heard her say 'i don't know how to formulate this'

7:32PM May 14
just want to write a book so good that all of my behavior is excusable

6:26AM May 16
slept ~3 sec and woke experiencing a distinct, real-seeming memory of me telling a stoic, native american man to 'leave my cars alone'

1:37PM May 22
thought 'i look too good to be doing this shit' while laying in fetal position on bedroom floor and crying

12:19PM May 22
feel like a broken-but-fixable robot whose owner can afford to replace me but hasn't yet

12:03AM May 26
feel like a weird, retarded sea urchin with an abnormally long neck who sees things ~6% slower than all other sea urchins

2:18AM May 30
imagined eddie murphy floating in a park with a turtle shell on his back

11:28AM Jun 4
~5 min after feeling 'amazing', began eating carbs, watching tv, and thinking 'hellish' thoughts in an earnestly involuntary-seeming manner

11:06AM Jun 12
imagined a 'droid x' with a 'mr. potato head' type face repeatedly banging its head against the wall, saying 'mown jah loh mon eselom'

11:04AM Jun 14
diarrhea anne frank

1:14AM Jun 18
just stood up, lost 'all control' of left leg and fell into an arcade game, making a loud noise and 'yelping' #xmenlivetweet

1:24AM Jun 18
man in theatre rhythmically 'yelped' 3x and i immediately assumed he was lonely and worked in a cubicle #xmenlivetweet

1:54AM Jun 18
thought i thought 'i can't feel my legs' 3x then realized an xman said it...#xmenlivetweet

11:15PM Jun 23
noticed myself re-thinking all emotional thoughts in a 'beyonce style vibrato' for an amount of time then kept doing it 'for fun,' alone

11:01AM Jun 25
feel like a 50 y/o man reflecting on his life in a severely detached/disinterested manner while sitting in his cubicle and staring

4:15AM Jun 26
closed my eyes and imagined a stoic, strong-seeming native american face moving slowly 'into my face'

4:18AM Jun 26
thought the bathroom fan was a radio playing a 'kiss-esque' song with lyrics 'let's go, oh yeah, put the belly on, i'm in the woods'

11:45AM Jul 1
'see you', as a typed salutation, seems weird/insane to me, but 'see ya' seems perfectly normal...

11:44PM Jul 5
if 100 people retweet this i'll earnestly try to rip my penis off in a video

3:54AM Jul 18
idly yearned for the universe to 'have a blanket' to cover me/my surroundings with when i'm awake at 5AM, alone, looking at facebook...

11:40AM Jul 22
feels like i'm breaking into random houses in 'broad daylight' and 'rummaging around' for 'happiness'

11:43AM Jul 27
can't remember what a living turkey looks like...

10:15AM Aug 4
want to express that 'despite how depraved/sad/mean i might seem, i'm actually, in fact, quite [something]'...

2:41PM Aug 4
saw an obese mom and 5x obese children in running outfits eating meatball subs around the trunk of their mini van

11:58PM Aug 7
thought 'pound time' excitedly while staring at a pile of muffins and a cake

10:27AM Aug 8
there are things i can change in my concrete reality to feel less bad but for some reason i feel completely unable to change them

12:19PM Aug 10
my brain feels like a firm, square container holding something rumored to be 'magical' but in reality is just weird and unwieldy

12:31PM Aug 16
seems like 'even my death' will be an untimely/annoying accident

1:27PM Aug 17
feel paralyzed by both 'feeling truly alone in the world' and 'being able to do anything because of being alone'...

6:53AM Aug 25
today is the first day of my freshman year of college

INTRO TO HUMAN COMMUNICA-TION

i get better grades when i give speeches that i don't prepare ahead of
time

i can't make simple decisions in the same way an infant can't make
simple decisions

i don't know what to do or why or how to do it

DORM ROOM TERROR

i feel terrified of living in a dorm

like, genuinely terrified of living in a dorm...

just imagined my wikipedia page saying 'died in a dorm'

seems terrible

'PHOTO BOOTH' VIDEO EMOTIONAL POEM

after watching an amount of 'photo booth' videos

i feel life as something massive yet light

a calmly emotional piece of oversized confetti

discarded in a dumpster

on a sunny day

alone

remembering pre-production, it's short yet undeniably important

past, the only thing

that ever really mattered

and i'm reminded of health, limited time, and, for some reason,

a little of school

10.10.11.
5:30AM

awake to watch the sun rise for the third night in a row

drinking coors banquet brand beer

in my dorm room

alone

vyvanse, hydroxyene, xanax, caffeine, nicotine, marijuana, alcohol

earlier i sat on a blanket in grass with mallory and aaron

later i went to a hipster bar then a gay bar then a hipster bar

tomorrow i will get my paycheck

try not to spend it all on drugs

try to believe in myself despite no one else believing in me

finally do some laundry

get my stupid fucking life in order

RAYMOND CARVER'S '*WHAT WE TALK ABOUT WHEN WE TALK ABOUT LOVE*' (THE STORY) OR DENNIS COOPER'S '*UGLY MAN*' (THE BOOK)

i want my body to transform into a complete, declarative sentence written using active voice and a prose style similar to raymond carver's 'what we talk about when we talk about love' (the story) or dennis cooper's 'ugly man' (the book) and i want the sentence to convey the sentiment 'we all have limited time' and 'honestly, i'm sorry'

GRANOLA
BAR
SORROW

stood in my parent's pantry for around six minutes while 'weakly
clutching' a granola bar

put it back on the shelf then walked away slowly while thinking what
seemed like nothing

THE
SOCIAL
NETWORK

the last scene of 'the social network' seemed really sweet

like, when he was repeatedly refreshing his ex-girlfriend's facebook
    page

i liked that a lot

11.13.92

the hand of life extends
as though to
greet me

then slaps me in the face repeatedly

11.15.10

the intense bleakness of an unrung steak

a retarded urge to yelp

watching 'hamlet' in english class

the teacher just yelled at someone for sleeping

i hate being alive

11.22.10

just laughed out loud re something in 'hamlet' in an unseemly manner

someone just laughed a 'booming' laugh

someone in 'hamlet' screamed

*

just ate a banana while thinking 'just ate a banana,' 'just ate a banana
next to two african americans' then 'this...as the poem'

*

watched a five-minute-long 'hamlet' soliloquy

*

art can just be like, the things i make for myself or my friends or
whatever

HAMLET
ASS
PANCAKES

just imagined myself standing, ripping the test i'm taking in half, screaming while waving my arms above my head, leaving the classroom, slamming the door, sitting with my back against a locker in the hallway, and crying hysterically into my hands

*

just looked around the room thinking something like 'k-pin...fucking...' then 'drug maniac' then 'cheating' then 'what the fuck...' then 'what the fuck is this shit' then 'gahh'

just felt the inside of my left pocket then thought about sam in an unexpectedly comforting manner

*

what are the long-term effects of touching my moustache so frequently

*

just stared at the test i'm taking with unfocused eyes thinking 'hamlet is belligerent' in a manner like i expressed that sentiment in an email before, or something

'PAPER PLANES' BY M.I.A.

keep thinking of the chorus of 'paper planes' by m.i.a.

but with the lyrics

'ain't nobody wanna get shot like that'

or...

no...

it was something...

something different....

like...noises...

like 'fooble fobble drooble drop'

or something...

EATING
DISORDER

having trouble discerning

whether or not i feel hungry

seems 'not hungry, but hungry'

or something

YOU GUYS KNOW SHRIMP, RIGHT? WELL SHRIMP, YOU KNOW, THEY KEEP EVERYTHING TO THEMSELVES. LIKE, THEY DON'T GIVE TO CHARITY OR ANYTHING. WELL THE OTHER DAY, MY FRIEND, HE TOLD ME, HE SAID 'YOU KNOW WHY SHRIMP ARE LIKE THAT, DON'TCHA?' I TOLD HIM, I SAID 'NO CLUE, WHY ARE THEY LIKE THAT?' HE TOLD ME, HE SAID 'BECAUSE THEY'RE *SHELLFISH*'

if you call someone because you want to talk to them, that is selfish

and selfish people suck

when i don't respond to a text

it's okay

to feel nothing

to look at a chair or a person and think

'a chair'

'a person'

it's okay

to stop acting a certain way and to not replace that way with another
way

it's okay

to take things

nothing is stolen and everything is stolen

nothing is returned and everything is returned

life is not fair trade

life is loss

or...

i mean...

nothing is gained or lost

or...

i don't know...

there is nothing i can give

nothing i can take

this is something i want you to know

i mean, i think it is

i feel tired, high, calm

caring is the same as not caring

because caring doesn't help or change anything

things that don't exist

just don't exist

or something

i kind of want to eat soft cookies but don't know if it's because i want
    to eat soft cookies or because the last time i was in this situation - on
    drugs and in my basement - i ate soft cookies with people i like but
    don't see often, which was fun

'AMERICAN PSYCHO'

just imagined my head as christian bale's head in 'american psycho'
boarding a plane, telling his butler 'when I die, chop my penis off and
send it to my biggest fan so they can suck it' then imagined 'stewie'
from 'family guy' sucking a floating penis

'SECOND MARRIAGE'

just imagined giving the same pair of shoes to my wife two years in a row as birthday presents then her saying 'you can't remember anything from the past year?' and me not being able to remember anything from the past year

CAN'T STOP THINKING THAT PEOPLE ARE PROBABLY INHERENTLY FUCKED AND OTHER THINGS ABOUT THE BLEAKNESS OF THE UNIVERSE

while shitting at school, i saw a 'domestic violence awareness' poster
on the back of the stall door with words like 'choking' and 'neglect'
and 'psychological' on it

i imagined cowboys on horses, drinking whiskey, smoking pipe tobacco

then thought something like 'look around the room...the chances of a
person knowing a person or a person in the room being addicted to
some sort of drug are...1/4...some high percentage...'

then imagined myself in scrubs, stroking my facial hair while thinking
about how everything everyone does is an attempt at ignoring or
forgetting the fact that they're awake or [some other awful thing]

POOPING
IN PUBLIC
RESTROOMS

most people seem to feel aversion toward pooping in public restrooms

but i like it

it feels good to leave a social situation

look at my cell phone

in the solitude of a bathroom stall

bare-assed on a toilet

letting it all out

knowing i will have to poop again at some point but also knowing that
soon, if only for a moment, the shit once within me will be gone

a broadened definition of poetry

a poem

HAIKU FOR POOPING DURING CLASS

everybody knows
i've been gone for like 10 min
pooping during class

SAD
AMERICANS

i feel so sad

this morning i woke up and immediately felt terrible

there wasn't a moment between sleeping and waking when i didn't feel
the acute ache of being alive

the unbearable agony of everything at once

the soul-sucking seconds of minutes, minutes of hours, hours of days,
days of weeks, weeks of months, months of years

oh my god

so stupid

i dreamt about mallory, brittany, tao, and noah. on the car ride to hang
out with them, i experienced feelings of fear that tao would 'take'
mallory 'from me' and that noah and brittany would leave us to be
alone together. at some point during the dream i looked through a
window and saw tao and noah holding hands outside in a field. i
looked to my right and saw mallory and brittany in the other room
touching each others breasts, looking at each other, smiling

this morning i didn't want to do drugs then did drugs after looking at the
internet

i feel like i can't do anything without drugs

any drug as long as it's a lot

or a combination

of drugs

and drugs

and drugs

and drugs

i feel so sad

a sad american

writing in my cell phone while pooping at school

APPLE
CIDER

feeling so retarded
staring out a window
at a nice-looking tree

navigating the internet
beneath warm blankets

fall in ohio

HAIKU
FOR
MONDAY
MORNING

mirror staring me
adderall and percocet
another week, here

I DON'T FEEL COMFORT-ABLE AROUND YOU ANYMORE

i don't feel comfortable when you say things like 'she walked right past me and didn't say hi,' implying that [person] 'shouldn't have' walked past you without saying hi and that it affected you emotionally

i would feel more comfortable if, instead of saying something but meaning something else, you said exactly what you meant, like 'her walking past me and not saying hi seemed inconsiderate and embarrassing to me, causing me to feel decreased levels of self-confidence due to my thought process in that specific moment'

then maybe i could say something like 'i'm sorry that you feel bad. it's possible that she didn't see you or didn't recognize you because it was dark or something. your bad feelings are being caused by an assumption that she had certain intentions which she may or may not have had, and since an assumption is something one makes, you can fix your negative feelings, feel better then move on'

not to lecture you or to 'prove a point' but to earnestly attempt to help you feel better

fundamentally

when sentences are purposely left open to interpretation of what was meant to be implied

miscommunications happen

then confusion

then bad feelings as a result of miscommunication and confusion

etc

UNBEARABLE

when i look at my face in the mirror

it's everybody ever looking at my face in the mirror

i'm listening to paul baribeau

before going to a paul baribeau show

ALLERGIC
TO
PEANUTS

i want to shrink into the size of a peanut and eat myself because i'm
   allergic to peanuts and i hate being alive

OLD
MAN
BACK

pain perpetuates itself;
happiness does not

concrete reality perceived in a specific manner causes negative thought
    processes
negative thought processes cause sadness
sadness causes escapism
escapism causes undesired effects in concrete reality
concrete reality perceived in a specific manner causes a negative
    thought process
etc

problems cause symptoms
and symptoms are assessed
to identify problems

i don't know

the only way to know things is to exclude information
via contexts and goals
but even then things are only known in terms of those contexts and
goals

no

i don't know

things seem terrible

yesterday i felt tired and sad

today i feel tired and sad

the definition of sadness is sadness

not the opposite of happiness

things seem terrible

i don't know

it feels possible to me that sadness exists

alone

because of chemicals or something

and not in the context of happiness

which seems devastating

and terrible

to me

or something

i don't know

Jordan Castro (b. 1992) is the author of YOUNG AMERICANS (Civil Coping Mechanisms, 2013) and *if i really wanted to feel happy i'd feel happy already* (Black Coffee Press, 2013). He is the author of KA-DIAN (hiphiphooray press, 2012), the co-author of 3 other chapbooks, and the author of 3 ebooks. He sings and plays guitar in *The Ohioans*. He has been "widely published" on the internet.

@jordan_castro
www.animalsorrow.com

Made in the USA
Charleston, SC
22 June 2015